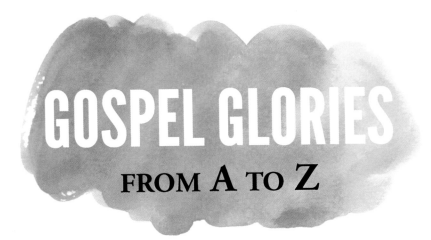

GOSPEL GLORIES

FROM A TO Z

Kelly Havrilla

ISBN-13: 978-0692947968
ISBN-10: 0692947965

Full Color Edition

Cover Design: Laura Schembre of Copper Street Design
www.copperstreetdesign.com

GCD Books is a ministry of Gospel-Centered Discipleship. Our purpose is to produce resources that make, mature, and multiply disciples of Jesus. Visit us at GCDiscipleship.com

GCD Books
Austin, TX

Printed in the United States of America.

TABLE OF CONTENTS

ACKNOWLEDGEMENTS

There have been so many who have influenced my walk with Jesus since the day God opened my eyes to the glory of his good news in Christ, but there are several who have so impacted my life for the sake of the gospel that I want to acknowledge them here.

First and foremost, I want to thank my dear husband David, who is my constant companion and friend. We have been partners in the gospel from the very first days in our journey of faith, and he has contributed immeasurably to this work. He has walked side by side with me through all that God in his providence has had for our lives.

I also want to thank four other men. The first is Dr. John MacArthur whose radio ministry led me to Christ as an atheist and who has shaped my theology through his numerous commentaries, books and audio sermons. The other three are my former pastors: Bill Barber, Rick Halfmann and Mark Morgan. Through their many years of pastoral dedication, preaching, teaching and mentoring, I have grown in grace and in my knowledge of biblical truth—to them I am forever indebted.

Finally, I want to thank Pastor Jeremy Writebol for his support and encouragement of this book, and for his preaching ministry that boldly, clearly and passionately explains the Scriptures, proclaims the glory of God, declares the gospel, and provides me with practical application week after week.

PREFACE

God made him who had no sin to be sin for us so that in him we might become the righteousness of God. — 2 Corinthians 5:21

"For God so loved the world that he gave his one and only Son" (Jn 3:16). That is the good news about Jesus Christ in a sentence, and that is the best news of all time for the entire world. The gospel, which means good news, is the centerpiece of the Christian message. It explains that although every person is separated from God because of sin, God in his justice, mercy, and love has made a way for us to be made right with him. And that way is remarkably simple—trusting in the person and work of Jesus Christ.

The Bible teaches that Jesus brought peace between God and man through his perfect life, sacrificial death on a cross, and resurrection from the grave. Jesus himself proclaimed in the Gospel of John, "I am the way, the truth and the life. No one comes to the Father except through me" (Jn. 14:6). This is an extraordinary claim. C.S. Lewis, Oxford scholar and author of the famous Chronicles of Narnia series, posed a compelling statement about Jesus. He said in view of all that Jesus did and said about himself, one cannot view him as merely an incredible teacher, a remarkable prophet, or an exceptionally moral man. He must be either a liar, a lunatic, or he is who he said he is—Lord of all.

It's a wonderfully amazing thing that we have the most credible and well-attested book of all time testifying about the life and works of Jesus—the Bible. Comprised of both Old and New Testaments with 66 books written by about 40 authors over a period of some 2000 years, the Bible has God's ultimate plan of redemption as its singular theme. It repeatedly points to Jesus as the only person qualified to accomplish the task. The Bible authoritatively and accurately records who Jesus was, what he did, what he said, what others thought of him, and how they reacted to his claims. His greatest claim is that he is the very Son of God, sent by his Father on a rescue mission to save people on planet earth. And that is indeed good news!

In a New Testament letter to the church in Corinth, the Apostle Paul wrote, "God made him who had no sin to be sin for us so that in him we might become the righteousness of God" (2 Cor. 5:21). This is the good news from the pen of the great apostle in concise form. God sent Jesus to earth to die for sins, and to rise again, so that those who trust in him can be forgiven of their sins and be declared righteous.

In the following pages, we will navigate our way through the alphabet of twenty-six gospel rich words; words which will enlighten, encourage and challenge us all. The gospel is the only true life-giving message in all the universe. I pray you learn it, believe it, and embrace it for yourself.

ATONEMENT

Atonement speaks of the reconciliation between God and man accomplished through the life, suffering, and sacrificial death of Jesus. To atone for sin is to appease God's wrath on sin. Jesus was the only one who could ever do this. He pleased God in every way. He was righteous in all that he did—in his life, and in his unjust death.

Because he was the Son of God and because he was sinless, Jesus was perfectly qualified to do what no other human could ever do—take on the wrath of God the Father on behalf of the sins of another. It is only through his atonement that anyone can be brought into a right relationship with God.

We are either pardoned or punished by God, depending on what we do with Jesus Christ. Christ's atonement allows God to pardon justly the sins of anyone who trusts in Jesus because he took the punishment we deserve and fully paid the price for all our sins.

VERSES TO REFLECT ON

My dear children, I write this to you so that you will not sin. But if anybody does sin, we have an advocate with the Father—Jesus Christ, the Righteous One. He is the atoning sacrifice for our sins, and not only for ours but also for the sins of the whole world.

1 John 2:1-2

For this reason he had to be made like them, fully human in every way, in order that he might become a merciful and faithful high priest in service to God, and that he might make atonement for the sins of the people.

Hebrews 2:17

This is how God showed his love among us: He sent his one and only Son into the world that we might live through him. This is love: not that we loved God, but that he loved us and sent his Son as an atoning sacrifice for our sins.

1 John 4:9-10

MEMORY VERSE

God presented Christ as a sacrifice of atonement, through the shedding of his blood—to be received by faith.

Romans 3:25

IN YOUR OWN WORDS: WHAT IS THE ATONEMENT?

_____

_____

_____

_____

_____

_____

_____

_____

_____

RESPONDING TO GOD IN PRAYER

_____

_____

_____

_____

_____

_____

_____

_____

BELIEVE

In the Bible, to "believe" is to trust, have faith in, or completely embrace something or someone. It is a conscious mental decision that affirms with certainty. It is not a passive sort of belief that acquiesces to simple facts. True biblical faith, because it is produced and accompanied by God's Spirit, dramatically alters the course of a convert's life.

For the believer, there is an enduring confidence and trust in Jesus Christ for a right standing before God. To believe in Jesus Christ means you agree and fully trust that he is everything he said he is, and that he is the only way to be made right with God. To believe in Jesus means to submit to God and to follow his ways.

To believe in Christ is to be "in Christ," and to receive the myriad of benefits accompanying that relationship. This status before God cannot be earned by doing good things and shunning bad things. The only way to God is to believe in Jesus Christ alone with enduring confidence and trust.

VERSES TO REFLECT ON

Abram believed the Lord, and he credited it to him as righteousness.

Genesis 15:6

For I am not ashamed of the gospel, because it is the power of God that brings salvation to everyone who believes: first to the Jew, then to the Gentile.

Romans 1:16

For God so loved the world that he gave his one and only Son, that whoever believes in him shall not perish but have eternal life.

John 3:16

Through him you believe in God, who raised him from the dead and glorified him, and so your faith and hope are in God.

1 Peter 1:21

MEMORY VERSE

If you declare with your mouth, "Jesus is Lord," and believe in your heart that God raised him from the dead, you will be saved.

Romans 10:9

IN YOUR OWN WORDS: WHAT DOES IT MEAN TO BELIEVE?

_____

_____

_____

_____

_____

_____

_____

RESPONDING TO GOD IN PRAYER

_____

_____

_____

_____

_____

_____

_____

CROSS

The cross of Christ is the focal point of God's plan of salvation from eternity past. Jesus' crucifixion at Calvary had been anticipated before God spoke the universe into existence. It is the place where every saint, past or present, today or far off in the future, receives the love and mercy of God.

At the cross of Christ, God unveils his character in diamond-like brilliance. It is where the repentant sinner sees God's holiness, love, grace, mercy, forgiveness, righteousness, wisdom, power, patience, justice and glory radiating from the face of Christ Jesus the Lord.

The cross was to the first century Romans a symbol of horrific death. To the Christian, it is a symbol of God's incredible salvation. In one of his letters, the Apostle Peter wrote these encouraging and powerful words applicable to believers in every generation: "He himself bore our sins in his body on the cross so that we might die to sins and live to righteousness" (1 Pet. 2:24).

VERSES TO REFLECT ON

And being found in appearance as a man, he humbled himself by becoming obedient to death—even death on a cross!
Philippians 2:8

When you were dead in your sins and in the uncircumcision of your flesh, God made you alive with Christ. He forgave us all our sins, having canceled the charge of our legal indebtedness, which stood against us and condemned us; he has taken it away, nailing it to the cross. And having disarmed the powers and authorities, he made a public spectacle of them, triumphing over them by the cross.
Colossians 2:13-15

For the joy set before him he endured the cross, scorning its shame, and sat down at the right hand of the throne of God.
Hebrews 12:2

MEMORY VERSE

For God was pleased to have all his fullness dwell in him, and through him to reconcile to himself all things, whether things on earth or things in heaven, by making peace through his blood, shed on the cross.
Colossians 1:19-20

IN YOUR OWN WORDS: WHY IS THE CROSS SO IMPORTANT?

_____

_____

_____

_____

_____

_____

_____

_____

RESPONDING TO GOD IN PRAYER

_____

_____

_____

_____

_____

_____

_____

_____

DEATH

From the disobedience of the very first humans came the certain reality of death. The Bible declares that we all die because we are sinners (Rom. 5:12). By contrast, Christ's death is unique and essentially different from any other death because he lived a sinless life. At the cross Jesus paid the penalty—not for his sin, but for ours. And when he rose from the dead, he conquered death for those he redeemed.

There is nothing more certain than death for every one of us. It is the curse of sin, and it will pursue us all the way to the grave. But Christ rose from the dead, and he rescues believers from death. Since he was without sin, death could not hold him. And all those that are "in Christ" will also rise from the dead to eternal life with God.

Death is the doorway to an eternal state—either eternal life with God in Christ, or eternal death without him in the lake of fire. Christ's death made eternal life a certainty for all who trust in him.

VERSES TO REFLECT ON

Very truly I tell you, whoever hears my word and believes him who sent me has eternal life and will not be judged but has crossed over from death to life.

John 5:24

But God raised him from the dead, freeing him from the agony of death, because it was impossible for death to keep its hold on him.

Acts 2:24

He was delivered over to death for our sins and was raised to life for our justification.

Romans 4:25

But we do see Jesus, who was made lower than the angels for a little while, now crowned with glory and honor because he suffered death, so that by the grace of God he might taste death for everyone.

Hebrew 2:9

But now he has reconciled you by Christ's physical body through death to present you holy in his sight, without blemish and free from accusation.

Colossians 1:22

MEMORY VERSE

For the wages of sin is death, but the gift of God is eternal life in Christ Jesus our Lord.

Romans 6:23

IN YOUR OWN WORDS: WHY IS THERE DEATH?

_____

_____

_____

_____

_____

_____

_____

_____

RESPONDING TO GOD IN PRAYER

_____

_____

_____

_____

_____

_____

_____

_____

Eternal

Jesus Christ is the eternal Son of God. He has no beginning or end; he is everlasting. He is the creator and sustainer of all things within time, including time itself. Since Jesus Christ is eternal and beyond time, by his very nature he is unchanging, because time does not have any influence on him. Therefore, whatever he says or does has validity for all time. Once we place our faith in Jesus, our salvation is secure for eternity. We can never lose our salvation because the one who purchased it is the one who insures it, and he is eternal—not to mention all powerful.

Our Savior is eternally consistent in character and never changes his mind, so our salvation is eternally secure. He will always be our advocate before God the Father. His providence will always result in our good, regardless of what happens to us.

What a comforting reality this is in a world of constant change and in continual turmoil, where relationships are fragile and fractured because of sin. Jesus Christ is forever the same.

VERSES TO REFLECT ON

Jesus Christ is the same yesterday and today and forever.
Hebrews 13:8

And this is the testimony: God has given us eternal life, and this life is in his Son. Whoever has the Son has life; whoever does not have the Son of God does not have life.
1 John 5:11-12

For my Father's will is that everyone who looks to the Son and believes in him shall have eternal life, and I will raise them up at the last day."
John 6:40

MEMORY VERSE

I write these things to you who believe in the name of Son of God so that you may know that you have eternal life.
1 John 5:13

IN YOUR OWN WORDS: DESCRIBE HOW JESUS IS ETERNAL.

_____

_____

_____

_____

_____

_____

_____

_____

RESPONDING TO GOD IN PRAYER

_____

_____

_____

_____

_____

_____

_____

_____

_____

FORGIVENESS

Forgiveness is a precious word. From forgiveness flows the joy of a restored relationship and the peace of reconciliation with God. Whether or not we are willing to admit or accept it, we are desperately in need of God's forgiveness. We need to be forgiven in order to be restored to a right relationship to God, and we also need to be righteous—perfectly righteous. There is only one person in all creation that can provide both for us—Jesus Christ. Our sin separates us from God. He is completely holy, utterly sinless, and perfect in every way. We are sinful, corrupt in motive, thought, action and word. Jesus Christ, because of his sinlessness, was able to do what no other person could do.

While he was dying on the cross, Jesus took on the wrath of God, the penalty for sin. That very act earned God's forgiveness for all who will come to Christ Jesus by faith. The beloved Apostle John wrote this in 1 John chapter two: "I am writing you, dear children, because your sins have been forgiven on account of his name" (1 Jn. 2:12). Believe in him, and be included in the family of all who are forgiven by God in Christ.

VERSES TO REFLECT ON

For he has rescued us from the dominion of darkness and brought us into the kingdom of the Son he loves, in whom we have redemption, the forgiveness of sins.
Colossians 1:13-14

Therefore, my friends, I want you to know that through Jesus the forgiveness of sins is proclaimed to you. Through him everyone who believes is set free from every sin, a justification you were not able to obtain under the law of Moses.
Acts 13:38-39

All the prophets testify about him that everyone who believes in him receives forgiveness of sins through his name.
Acts 10:43

MEMORY VERSE

In him we have redemption through his blood, the forgiveness of sins, in accordance with the riches of God's grace that he lavished on us.
Ephesians 1:7-8

IN YOUR OWN WORDS: HOW IS GOD'S FORGIVENESS OBTAINED?

_____

_____

_____

_____

_____

_____

_____

RESPONDING TO GOD IN PRAYER

_____

_____

_____

_____

_____

_____

_____

_____

GRACE

Amazing grace, how sweet the sound! Grace is receiving kindness, mercy, and favor from another when it is not deserved. For Christians and non-Christians alike, God's grace is abundant and includes every blessing we enjoy from his hand—family, friends, health, life, talents, shelter, a beautiful sunset, rain for our crops, food on the table, the list goes on and on. We certainly do not deserve God's favor in all the blessings he bestows on us, but he provides them nonetheless because of his amazing grace.

In relation to the gospel, God's grace means receiving his salvation instead of his justice, wrath, and punishment. God's grace cannot be earned nor procured in any way. Although we do not deserve God's favor and could never earn it, we can receive it by faith alone in Jesus Christ alone. The Bible says where sin increased, grace increased all the more (Rom. 5:20). Sin has never and will never frustrate God's plan of salvation. God is the eternal king of all creation, and his grace is boundless. For the believer in Christ, God's grace does not end at salvation; it extends throughout all of life and into eternity.

VERSES TO REFLECT ON

[S]o that, having been justified by his grace, we might become heirs having the hope of eternal life.

Titus 3:7

[A]nd all are justified freely by his grace through the redemption that came by Christ Jesus.

Romans 3:24

And if by grace, then it cannot be based on works; if it were, grace would no longer be grace.

Romans 11:6

MEMORY VERSE

For it is by grace you have been saved, through faith—and this is not from yourselves, it is the gift of God not by works, so that no one can boast.

Ephesians 2:8-9

IN YOUR OWN WORDS: WHAT IS GRACE?

_____

_____

_____

_____

_____

_____

_____

_____

RESPONDING TO GOD IN PRAYER

_____

_____

_____

_____

_____

_____

_____

_____

_____

Hope

Hope. Isn't that word soothing balm for the soul? Especially in difficult times, hope may be all we have to hang on to. Yet sometimes, no matter how hard we hope for a certain outcome, it doesn't happen and it feels like all hope is lost. However, when the Bible speaks of hope, it speaks of certainty because it is grounded in someone trustworthy, faithful, and true—the King of kings over all creation—Jesus Christ. The hope of the Christian is grounded in him. Eternity with God is a certainty for all who trust in Jesus because of who he is and what he has done on the cross. The things and people of this world will always disappoint, but Jesus Christ will not.

Difficulties are sure to come, but God has provided a hope in the gospel that reaches beyond every difficulty. This hope is available to all who place their trust in Jesus Christ. He is the certain anchor for the soul throughout life's greatest challenges and deepest sorrows, in the darkest trials and in seasons of debilitating pain. What a comfort it is to know that because of what he endured, Jesus understands our great need for hope, a hope that transcends this world.

VERSES TO REFLECT ON

No one whose hope is in you will ever be put to shame.
Psalm 25:3

[A] faith and knowledge resting on the hope of eternal life, which God, who does not lie, promised before the beginning of time.
Titus 1:2

To them God has chosen to make known among the Gentiles the glorious riches of this mystery which is Christ in you, the hope of glory.
Colossians 1:27

Now faith is being sure of what we hope for and certain of what we do not see.
Hebrews 11:1

MEMORY VERSE

May the God of hope fill you with all joy and peace as you trust in him, so that you may overflow with hope by the power of the Holy Spirit.
1 Thessalonians 4:7

IN YOUR OWN WORDS: WHAT IS HOPE GROUNDED IN AND WHY?

_____

_____

_____

_____

_____

_____

_____

_____

RESPONDING TO GOD IN PRAYER

_____

_____

_____

_____

_____

_____

IMPUTE

To impute means to credit or attribute something to a person to whom it doesn't belong. As far as the gospel and the redemption of humanity are concerned, there are three imputations that have eternal consequences. The first happened at the dawn of humanity in the garden of Eden. When Adam sinned, his sin was imputed to every human being that has ever existed (theolgians refer to this concept as "original sin"), except one—Jesus Christ.

The second and third imputations take place when a person places their faith in Jesus Christ. At that very moment, the person's sin is imputed to Jesus because he bore the weight of the world's sin through his sacrificial death on the cross. Simultaneously, Christ's righteousness is credited to their account. Imputation is, therefore, a word drenched in God's grace. God treats the believer as though Christ's righteousness is actually theirs! And in God's eternal courtroom, the verdict is "not guilty" for all who by repentant faith have received Christ as Lord and have his righteousness as theirs.

VERSES TO REFLECT ON

For just as through the disobedience of the one man (Adam) the many were made sinners, so also through the obedience of the one man (Jesus) the many will be made righteous.
Romans 5:19

What does Scripture say? "Abraham believed God, and it was credited to him as righteousness." Now to the one who works, wages are not credited as a gift but as an obligation. However, to the one who does not work but trusts God who justifies the ungodly, their faith is credited as righteousness.
Romans 4:3-4

He himself bore our sins in his body on the tree, so that we might die to sins and live for righteousness.
1 Peter 2:24

Christ redeemed us from the curse of the law by becoming a curse for us.
Galatians 3:13

MEMORY VERSE

For just as through the disobedience of the one man the many were made sinners, so also through the obedience of the one man the many will be made righteous.
Romans 5:19

IN YOUR OWN WORDS: WHAT DOES IT MEAN THAT YOUR SIN WAS IMPUTED TO CHRIST, AND HIS RIGHTEOUSNESS WAS IMPUTED TO YOU?

_____

_____

_____

_____

_____

_____

_____

_____

RESPONDING TO GOD IN PRAYER

_____

_____

_____

_____

_____

_____

_____

_____

_____

JESUS

Though his ministry lasted only three short years, Jesus' impact on the world has been immeasurable. What he said about himself was extraordinary. He claimed to be the Son of God, to be the only way to God the Father, and to have come to earth to save sinners. His teachings, miracles, resurrection and ascension verify that Jesus is exactly who he said he was. The writers of Scripture call him: Emmanuel (God with us), the Holy One, the Savior, King of kings, the Lamb of God, the Way, the Truth and the Life.

These titles provide only a glimpse into his greatness. Jesus is the only way to God and the only source of eternal life. Jesus lived a completely sinless life, died an obedient death, was raised from the dead as proof of his righteousness and God's acceptance of his sacrifice, and is now seated at the right hand of God the Father. He is fully God and fully man; therefore, he can represent mankind perfectly to God the Father. God declares the believer righteous, not by the worthiness of his faith, but by the worthiness of the one in whom he has faith. Jesus Christ is God's solution to man's most significant problem—sin.

VERSES TO REFLECT ON

Now this is eternal life; that they may know you, the only true God, and Jesus Christ, whom you have sent.
John 17:3

[F]ixing our eyes on Jesus, the pioneer and perfecter of faith. For the joy set before him he endured the cross, scorning its shame, and sat down at the right hand of the throne of God.
Hebrews 12:2

Therefore, God exalted him to the highest place and gave him the name that is above every name, that at the name of Jesus every knee should bow, in heaven and on earth and under the earth, and acknowledge that Jesus Christ is Lord, to the glory of God the Father.
Philippians 2:9-11

MEMORY VERSE

The Son is the image of the invisible God, the firstborn over all creation. For in him all things were created: things in heaven and on earth, visible and invisible, whether thrones or powers or rulers or authorities; all things have been created through him and for him. He is before all things, and in him all things hold together.
Colossians 1:15-17

IN YOUR OWN WORDS: WHO IS JESUS?

_____

_____

_____

_____

_____

_____

_____

_____

_____

_____

RESPONDING TO GOD IN PRAYER

_____

_____

_____

_____

_____

_____

_____

_____

_____

KING

"King" is a term that denotes royalty. A king is sovereign and his kingdom is ruled by his decisions. Jesus Christ is the King of every king, and King of believers. The difference between a human king and Jesus Christ is that Jesus is the ultimate loving and merciful servant-king. He laid down his life for everyone in his kingdom. He desires willing obedience and voluntary submission to his rule. Believers are eager to submit to him not only because of what he has done for them, but also because he has enabled them by gifting them with the promised Holy Spirit who empowers and encourages them in their walk with Christ.

King Jesus came once to give his life as a ransom for many. He will come back again to vanquish all that oppose him and to gather everyone who loves him and bring them joyfully into the eternal kingdom he has prepared for them. In the Book of Revelation, the Apostle John sees the heavens open with great magnificence and glory, and Jesus in all his glory is revealed. He is the one Faithful and True. He is the Word of God, the Lord of lords, and the King of kings.

VERSES TO REFLECT ON

"Do not be afraid, Daughter Zion; see, your king is coming, seated on a donkey's colt."
John 12:15

"You are a king, then!" said Pilate. Jesus answered, "You say that I am a king. In fact, the reason I was born and came into the world is to testify to the truth. Everyone on the side of truth listens to me."
John 18:37

For to us a child is born, to us a son is given, and the government will be on his shoulders. And he will be called Wonderful Counselor, Mighty God, Everlasting Father, Prince of Peace.
Isaiah 9:6

MEMORY VERSE

On his robe and on his thigh he has this name written: KING OF KINGS AND LORD OF LORDS.
Revelation 19:16

IN YOUR OWN WORDS: WHAT KIND OF KING IS JESUS?

_____

_____

_____

_____

_____

_____

_____

_____

_____

RESPONDING TO GOD IN PRAYER

_____

_____

_____

_____

_____

_____

_____

_____

_____

LOVE

The Bible declares that God is love. God shows his love in many ways to everyone. However, he also shows his love to all people in the most profound way, a way that will endure throughout all eternity—offering salvation through faith in Jesus Christ. God demonstrated his great love for us by having his Son die on the cross for those who are utterly unworthy of his grace.

At the cross, God loved believers by punishing his sinless Son for our sins. His love has created a way to be restored into a right relationship with God through his Son Jesus. God's love is unique in that he does not look for value in a person in order to love them; he literally imparts value to people by loving them.

The world does not love this way; it looks for value first before paying any attention, let alone loving. But God's love is altogether different. He loved us by taking care of our sin problem even while the world was ignoring, even hating him. This is the essence of true love.

VERSES TO REFLECT ON

But God demonstrates his own love for us in this: While we were still sinners Christ died for us.

Romans 5:8

[N]either height nor depth, nor anything else in all creation, will be able to separate us from the love of God that is in Christ Jesus our Lord.

Romans 8:39

But because of his great love for us, God, who is rich in mercy, made us alive with Christ even when we were dead in transgressions—it is by grace you have been saved.

Ephesians 2:4

MEMORY VERSE

For God so loved the world that he gave his one and only Son, that whoever believes in him shall not perish but have eternal life.

John 3:16

IN YOUR OWN WORDS: HOW WOULD YOU DESCRIBE TRUE LOVE?

_____

_____

_____

_____

_____

_____

_____

_____

_____

RESPONDING TO GOD IN PRAYER

_____

_____

_____

_____

_____

_____

_____

_____

MEDIATOR

A mediator is one who intervenes between two conflicting parties in order to bring reconciliation and peace. One of humanity's greatest needs is to have a mediator who can represent them before God. Whether we admit it or not, we are in conflict with God. Many are certainly sincere with their intentions and efforts to try to please God, but our works never have been and never will be good enough to gain favor with God. Even in the Old Testament, the purpose of God's Law was never to earn God's grace.

The Law provided a standard for living, to restrain sin, and to draw us to God for his grace and mercy. The way to God has never been through self-effort. Mankind has always needed a mediator, and Christ has always been the mediator between sinful people and a holy God. Jesus mediates for the sinner from the very beginning of their faith journey. He intercedes for the believer from the moment the sinner hears the gospel and responds in repentance and faith until he or she safely enters into the presence of God through death. What a Savior!

VERSES TO REFLECT ON

For this reason Christ is the mediator of a new covenant, that those who are called may receive the promised eternal inheritance—now that he has died as a random to set them free from the sins committed under the first covenant.
Hebrews 9:15

No one can redeem the life of another or give to God a ransom for them—the ransom for a life is costly, no payment is ever enough.
Psalm 49:7-8

[J]ust as the Son of Man did not come to be served, but to serve, and to give his life as a ransom for many.
Matthew 20:28

MEMORY VERSE

For there is one God and one mediator between God and men, the man Christ Jesus, who gave himself as a ransom for all men—the testimony given in its proper time.
1 Timothy 2:5-6

IN YOUR OWN WORDS: HOW IS JESUS A MEDIATOR FOR BELIEVERS?

_____

_____

_____

_____

_____

_____

_____

_____

RESPONDING TO GOD IN PRAYER

_____

_____

_____

_____

_____

_____

_____

_____

Narrow

In the Gospel of Matthew, Jesus tells the crowds to enter through the narrow gate that leads to eternal life, because the gate that leads to destruction is wide. When Jesus himself warns that the way to God is narrow, this ought to cause us to sit up and take notice. Countless people want to believe that there are many avenues to God, but God is the one who ultimately decides how we may come to him. And God's clear declaration throughout Scripture is that the only way to him is through the Savior, his Son Jesus Christ.

Though the path to him is narrow, God has not complicated it with tradition or works. It is by simple faith in Christ that we are brought into a right relationship with God. Salvation is by faith alone, in Christ alone—these are truths preached and defended by believers down through the ages, sometimes with their very lives. Jesus is the only way; he is the only path that leads to God the Father and to heaven. For a world lost and dying in sin, Jesus is the only cure, the only chance, the only hope.

VERSES TO REFLECT ON

Enter through the narrow gate. For wide is the gate and broad is the road that leads to destruction, and many enter through it. But small is the gate and narrow the road that leads to life, and only a few find it.

Matthew 7:13-14

He said to them, "Make every effort to enter through the narrow door, because many, I tell you, will try to enter and will not be able to."

Luke 13:24

Salvation is found in no one else, for there is no other name under heaven given to men by which we must be saved.

Acts 4:12

MEMORY VERSE

Jesus answered, "I am the way and the truth and the life. No one comes to the Father except through me."

John 14:6

IN YOUR OWN WORDS: IN WHAT SENSE IS THE WAY TO GOD NARROW?

_____

_____

_____

_____

_____

_____

_____

_____

RESPONDING TO GOD IN PRAYER

_____

_____

_____

_____

_____

_____

_____

ONCE

Christ died "once for all." His death was in the distant future for Old Testament believers and long ago for believers today. Yet what he accomplished at Calvary paid for the sins of every believer—past, present and even those to come, until whenever God the Father has determined the time of Jesus' return. As Jesus hung on the cross, he said, "It is finished." As far as works are concerned, there is nothing further that needs to be done regarding our salvation. "Jesus paid it all, all to him we owe!"

In the Old Testament times, the priests would offer sacrifice after sacrifice, year after year, for centuries. The sacrificial system was an ever-present reminder of the severity of sin. But it was also a reminder of God's mercy and the promise of the Messiah who would end the sacrificial system with one final and absolutely perfect sacrifice. One sacrifice; the righteous for the unrighteous, and the resurrection validated all that Jesus said and did throughout his sinless life and death.

VERSES TO REFLECT ON

[S]o Christ was sacrificed once to take away the sins of many people; and he will appear a second time, not to bear sin but to bring salvation to those who are waiting for him.
Hebrews 9:28

For the death he died, he died to sin once for all; but the life he lives, he lives in God.
Romans 6:10

Because by one sacrifice he has made perfect forever those who are being made holy.
Hebrews 10:14

MEMORY VERSE

For Christ died for sins once for all, the righteous for the unrighteous to bring you to God.
1 Peter 3:18

IN YOUR OWN WORDS: WHY DID JESUS ONLY NEED TO DIE ONCE FOR ALL SIN?

_____

_____

_____

_____

_____

_____

_____

_____

_____

RESPONDING TO GOD IN PRAYER

_____

_____

_____

_____

_____

_____

_____

_____

_____

Passover

The Old Testament Passover is an incredible illustration and foreshadowing of the cross. Moses was spokesman and prophet for the people of Israel to Egypt's Pharaoh. He demanded the release of his enslaved people, but time after time Pharaoh defaulted on his promises to release Israel. God responded with a series of plagues, the tenth of which was death. All firstborn males, human and livestock, died except for those in any household where the blood of a sacrificial lamb was on the sides and tops of the door frames. For these houses the angel of death did "pass over."

Jesus Christ himself is the ultimate sacrificial lamb to which the Passover event pointed. For everyone who trusts in Jesus, God's judgment of eternal death passes over that believer because Christ took God's wrath upon himself at the cross, shedding his blood for believers. Are you trusting in the sacrificial death and the glorious resurrection of Christ? Will the righteous judgment of God pass over you because of your trust in his sacrificial lamb? It is the only way to be made right with God, to have peace with him, and to have eternal life—don't wait any longer!

VERSES TO REFLECT ON

Then Moses summoned all the elders of Israel and said to them, "Go at once and select the animals for your families and slaughter the Passover Lamb. ... When the Lord goes through the land to strike down the Egyptians, he will see the blood on the top and sides of the doorframe and will pass over that doorway, and he will not permit the destroyer to enter your houses and strike you down.
Exodus 12:21, 23

The next day John saw Jesus coming toward him and said, "Look, the Lamb of God, who takes away the sin of the world"!
John 1:29

For you know that it was not with perishable things such as silver or gold that you were redeemed from the empty way of life handed down to you from your ancestors, but with the precious blood of Christ, a lamb without blemish or defect.
1 Peter 1:18–19

MEMORY VERSE

For Christ, our Passover lamb, has been sacrificed.
1 Corinthians 5:7

IN YOUR OWN WORDS: DESCRIBE THE PASSOVER.

_____

_____

_____

_____

_____

_____

_____

_____

_____

_____

RESPONDING TO GOD IN PRAYER

_____

_____

_____

_____

_____

_____

_____

_____

QUICKEN

To quicken is to make alive, to receive life. It refers to the spiritual life given to those who place their faith in Jesus Christ. We are all born spiritually dead. Our lives are centered on ourselves, even if we are sincerely trying to pursue God and earn his favor through all our efforts. But through the gospel of Christ proclaimed, and the work of God opening the heart of the hearer, spiritual life is breathed into believers. They have been raised from their spiritual deadness, and they are born again by the power of the Holy Spirit. They are made alive, or quickened, together with Christ.

Being born again is accompanied by a new nature — a new heart, a new King, new desires, a new thirst for God's Word, a new sensitivity to sin, a new ability to love, a new view of the world, a new vision, and a new mission for life. This new spiritual life sends the believer on a lifelong journey to know God more and more, and to be transformed ever closer to the image of Christ to the glory of God.

VERSES TO REFLECT ON

For you have been born again, not of perishable seed, but of imperishable, through the living and enduring word of God.
1 Peter 1:23

For as in Adam all die, so in Christ all will be made alive.
1 Corinthians 15:22

When you were dead in your sins and in the uncircumcision of your flesh, God made you alive with Christ. He forgave us all our sins.
Colossians 2:13

But when the kindness and love of God our Savior appeared, he saved us, not because of righteous things we had done, but because of his mercy. He saved us through the washing of rebirth and renewal by the Holy Spirit, whom he poured out on us generously through Jesus Christ our Savior, so that, having been justified by his grace, we might become heirs having the hope of eternal life.
Titus 3:4–7

MEMORY VERSE

Jesus replied, "Very truly I tell you, no one can see the kingdom of God unless they are born again.
John 3:3

IN YOUR OWN WORDS: HOW IS A PERSON QUICKENED?

_____

_____

_____

_____

_____

_____

_____

_____

_____

_____

RESPONDING TO GOD IN PRAYER

_____

_____

_____

_____

_____

_____

_____

_____

Righteousness

Righteousness is the character quality of being right according to God's holy standard. Simply stated, it is glorifying God with our lives as perfectly as Jesus did. This high and holy quality of righteousness applies to will, motive, thought, action and word. It is an attribute that we must possess in order to be justified by God. It is unattainable in and of ourselves. Why? Because every part of our being is infected and influenced by sin.

We cannot be as perfect as Jesus. Consider the following things that many religious people would say if asked why God should accept them: I am a good person, I give money to a church, I read the Bible, I was baptized, I help my neighbors, and on and on it goes. Every sentence starts with "I"! Does anyone do any of these things as perfectly as Jesus would? Of course not!

But here's the fantastic news of the gospel - at the point of saving faith, the sins of the Christian are transferred to Christ (and therefore punished by God), and are forgiven. At the same moment, Christ's righteousness is credited to the Christian, and the believer is declared righteous by God. Trust in Christ alone, and let His righteousness be your righteousness.

VERSES TO REFLECT ON

But when the kindness and love of God our Savior appeared, he saved us not because of righteous things we had done, but because of his mercy.

Titus 3:4-5

But whatever was to my profit I now consider loss for the sake of Christ. What is more, I consider everything a loss compared to the surpassing greatness of knowing Christ Jesus my Lord, for whose sake I have lost all things. I consider them rubbish, that I may gain Christ not having a righteousness of my own that comes from the law, but that which is through faith in Christ—the righteousness that comes from God and is by faith.

Philippians 3:7-9

But if Christ is in you, your body is dead because of sin, yet your spirit is alive because of righteousness.

Romans 8:10

MEMORY VERSE

This righteousness from God comes through faith in Jesus Christ to all who believe.

Romans 3:22

IN YOUR OWN WORDS: HOW DO WE OBTAIN RIGHTEOUSNESS?

_____

_____

_____

_____

_____

_____

_____

_____

_____

RESPONDING TO GOD IN PRAYER

_____

_____

_____

_____

_____

_____

_____

_____

Salvation

Salvation is the deliverance from the power and penalty of sin. It is the deliverance from eternal death at the moment of saving faith. It is a very precious gift which keeps on giving throughout all eternity. Salvation occurs when a sinner repents of sin and confesses Jesus as Lord and Savior. But salvation is not some kind of insurance policy that is procured only to escape the fires of hell. Salvation is much more than being rescued from the consequences of sin; it is the beginning of a new life and a new relationship with God. Salvation is not merely future tense; it starts at the moment of faith.

In John 17:3, Jesus said, "Now this is eternal life: that they may know you, the only true God and Jesus Christ whom you have sent." For the believer, salvation is a love relationship between God and his child, forever indebted to a loving, gracious, and merciful Father. And for the believer, the entirety of life, and life ever after, is all about loving and glorifying his God and Savior.

VERSES TO REFLECT ON

Now, brothers I want to remind you of the gospel I preached to you, which you received and on which you have taken your stand. By this gospel you are saved, if you hold firmly to the word I preached to you. Otherwise, you have believed in vain.
1 Corinthians 15:1-2

But these are written that you may believe that Jesus is the Christ, the Son of God, and that by believing you may have life in his name.
John 20:31

And everyone who calls on the name of the Lord will be saved.
Acts 2:21

For the Son of Man came to seek and to save what was lost.
Luke 19:10

MEMORY VERSE

That if you confess with your mouth, "Jesus is Lord," and believe in your heart that God raised him from the dead, you will be saved.

Romans 10:9

IN YOUR OWN WORDS: HOW IS A PERSON SAVED?

_____
_____
_____
_____
_____
_____
_____
_____
_____
_____
_____

RESPONDING TO GOD IN PRAYER

_____
_____
_____
_____
_____
_____
_____
_____
_____

TRUTH

"What is truth?" Pilate retorted when Jesus said that he came to testify to the truth. Knowing truth is paramount. We need the truth about all things in life to make the best and wisest decisions. And here's the truth—all the areas of life and reality have laws. There are physical laws, governmental laws, social laws, and so on. To ignore, disbelieve or disobey these laws have consequences. For example, if I were to disbelieve the law of gravity and jump off a twenty-story building, I would have a newfound belief in that law, at least for a few seconds.

The consequences in the spiritual realm are even more dire, which makes knowing spiritual truth vital. Here, Jesus is our trustworthy guide. Not only did he say that he came to testify to the truth, he said, "I am the truth." Jesus testified to the God of the Bible, to the authority of the Old Testament, and he promised the apostles the gift of the Holy Spirit who would remind them what to write.

So the Bible is our source of spiritual truth, and this is where we find the magnificence of the gospel conveyed and illustrated from cover to cover.

VERSES TO REFLECT ON

They exchanged the truth of God for a lie, and worshiped and served created things rather than the Creator—who is forever to be praised. Amen.

Romans 1:25

He chose to give us birth through the word of truth, that we might be a kind of firstfruits of all he created.

James 1:18

And you also were included in Christ when you heard the word of truth, the gospel of your salvation. Having believed you were marked in him with a seal, the promised Holy Spirit.

Ephesians 1:13

MEMORY VERSE

For the law was given through Moses, grace and truth came through Jesus Christ.

John 1:17

IN YOUR OWN WORDS: WHAT IS TRUTH AND HOW DO WE GET IT?

_____

_____

_____

_____

_____

_____

_____

_____

RESPONDING TO GOD IN PRAYER

_____

_____

_____

_____

_____

_____

_____

_____

UNCONDITIONAL

Without condition, unqualified, no strings attached—that's what unconditional means, and that describes God's love to those in Christ. His love never changes and is independent of anything the believer has done, is doing or will ever do. God calls and draws men to himself, and he freely gives the gifts of faith, repentance and eternal life. There is nothing about the recipient that earns or deserves the favor of God.

What God gives, he gives freely. God's salvation, which comes through the hearing and receiving of the gospel, is based on his love, grace and mercy. The only reason the gift of salvation can be offered at all has nothing whatsoever to do with us. Even faith itself is a gift from God. It is only because of the cross that God can offer the gift of salvation, unconditionally bestowed from the throne room of love.

And the relationship that starts unconditionally remains unconditional. In other words, the believer did not do anything to earn salvation, nor can he do anything to keep it. It is all by God's grace from beginning to end, and he who began a good work will be faithful to complete it.

VERSES TO REFLECT ON

For I am convinced that neither death nor life, neither angels nor demons, neither the present nor the future, not any powers, neither height nor depth, not anything else in all creation, will be able to separate us from the love of God that is in Christ Jesus our Lord.

Romans 8:38-39

May God himself, the God peace, sanctify you through and through. May your whole spirit, soul and body be kept blameless at the coming of our Lord Jesus Christ. The one who calls you is faithful and he will do it.

1 Thessalonians 5:23-24

Let us draw near to God with a sincere heart and with the full assurance that faith brings, having our hearts sprinkled to cleanse us from a guilty conscience and having our bodies washed with pure water. Let us hold unswervingly to the hope we profess, for he who promised is faithful.

Hebrews 10:22-23

MEMORY VERSE

I give them eternal life, and they shall never perish; no one can snatch them out of my hand. My Father, who has given them to me, is greater than all; no one can snatch them out of my Father's hand.

John 10:28-29

IN YOUR OWN WORDS: WHAT DOES GOD PROVIDE UNCONDITIONALLY?

_____

_____

_____

_____

_____

_____

_____

_____

RESPONDING TO GOD IN PRAYER

_____

_____

_____

_____

_____

_____

_____

_____

Victory

Victory is what Christ had over Satan, sin, and death when he died and rose again. No one else in the history of the world could ever completely conquer these devastating enemies of humanity. However, for those who are "in Christ" (those who are spiritually alive because of their wholehearted trust in all that Christ is and has done on their behalf), there is victory over these adversaries. In this life, there is ever-increasing victory empowered by the Holy Spirit, the Word of God, prayer and the fellowship of the church. In the life to come, there is complete victory.

The Bible says that "when we see him," that is Christ, "we will be like him, because we will see him as he is." At death, God will purify the believer completely. There will be no more sin nature and no more sinning. We will be like Christ in that way. The faithful will be made perfectly righteous by God—they will be glorified, and the Christian will spend all of his or her victorious eternity glorifying God and enjoying his holy presence.

VERSES TO REFLECT ON

This is love for God; to obey his commands. And his commands are not burdensome, for everyone born of God overcomes the world. This is the victory that has overcome the world, even our faith.

1 John 5:3-4

Dear friends, now we are children of God, and what we will be has not yet been made known. But we know that when Christ appears, we shall be like him, for we shall see him as he is.

1 John 3:2

MEMORY VERSE

But thanks be to God! He gives us the victory through our Lord Jesus Christ.

1 Corinthians 15:57

IN YOUR OWN WORDS: HOW DO WE GET VICTORY IN OUR LIVES?

_____

_____

_____

_____

_____

_____

_____

_____

_____

RESPONDING TO GOD IN PRAYER

_____

_____

_____

_____

_____

_____

_____

_____

Wisdom

True wisdom is applying biblical truth in a way that pleases God. Facts alone do not make us wise, even if we have an encyclopedic brain. The Apostle Paul describes wisdom in the book of Philippians:

> *And this is my prayer: that your love may abound more and more in knowledge and depth of insight, so that you may be able to discern what is best and may be pure and blameless for the day of Christ, filled with the fruit of righteousness that comes through Jesus Christ—to the glory and praise of God.*

Thus, wisdom (knowledge and depth of insight) is visible through ever-abounding love, which produces godly character and righteous deeds so that God may be glorified. Real wisdom cannot be attained outside of a relationship with Christ because it requires a desire for biblical truth and a life that is pleasing to God.

Wise application of biblical truth not only requires a relationship with Christ, but prayer, the fellowship of the church, and the enabling of the Holy Spirit. God mightily uses wise believers because they are the ones whose lives are most closely aligned with Jesus Christ, their Lord and Savior.

VERSES TO REFLECT ON

My purpose is that they may be encouraged in heart and united in love so that they may have the full riches of complete understanding, in order that they may know the mystery of God, namely Christ, in whom are hidden all the treasures of wisdom and knowledge.

Colossians 2:2-3

If any of you lacks wisdom he should ask God, who gives generously to all without finding fault, and it will be given to him.

James 1:5

All this also comes from the Lord Almighty, wonderful in counsel and magnificent in wisdom.

Isaiah 28:29

MEMORY VERSE

The fear of the Lord is the beginning of wisdom; all who follow his precepts have good understanding. To him belongs eternal praise.

Psalms 111:10

IN YOUR OWN WORDS: HOW IS TRUE WISDOM ATTAINED?

_____

_____

_____

_____

_____

_____

_____

_____

_____

RESPONDING TO GOD IN PRAYER

_____

_____

_____

_____

_____

_____

_____

_____

_____

Xenos

"Xenos" is the Greek word for "stranger." In Hebrews 11, the author speaks of the Old Testament faithful "admitting they were foreigners and strangers on earth" as they awaited the promises of God. They knew what God had in store for them was very different from the world around them. We see a similar idea in Paul's letter to the Philippians where he writes, "But our citizenship is in heaven. And we eagerly await a Savior from there, the Lord Jesus Christ." This world is not our home and Christians down through the centuries have longingly awaited the return of their Lord.

Followers of Christ are aliens on earth while our true home and most precious relationship lies elsewhere. But the believer has a high and holy calling as a foreigner here—as an ambassador on this planet—to faithfully represent Christ on behalf of their triune God and King. Believers are on this planet on a rescue mission to a people in dire need. We are here on special ops to go out into the world, to proclaim the good news and to make disciples for the glory of our everlasting King of kings.

VERSES TO REFLECT ON

All this is from God, who reconciled us to himself through Christ and gave us the ministry of reconciliation: that God was reconciling the world to himself in Christ, not counting men's sins against them. And he has committed to us the message of reconciliation. We are therefore Christ's ambassadors, as though God were making his appeal through us.
2 Corinthians 5:18-20

Consequently, you are no longer foreigners and aliens, but fellow citizens with God's people and members of God's household, built on the foundation of the apostles and prophets, with Christ Jesus himself as the chief cornerstone.
Ephesians 2:19-20

MEMORY VERSE

Dear friends, I urge you, as aliens and strangers in the world, to abstain from sinful desires, which war against your soul.
1 Peter 2:11

IN YOUR OWN WORDS: IN WHAT SENSE IS A BELIEVER A STRANGER ON EARTH?

_____

_____

_____

_____

_____

_____

_____

_____

RESPONDING TO GOD IN PRAYER

_____

_____

_____

_____

_____

_____

_____

_____

Yoke

A yoke is something that joins or binds together. A common way to use a yoke is to join two oxen together so they can work as a team. Jesus employs this agricultural imagery in Matthew 11:29-30 when he says, "Take my yoke upon you and learn from me, for I am gentle and humble in heart, and you will find rest for your souls. For my yoke is easy and my burden is light."

Come to the Lord Jesus and fear not his yoke. His gospel delivers people from wrath and guilt, sin and Satan, and provides them with new life and eternal purpose. He reconciles them with their God and Father, gives them a new capacity to love, the indwelling Holy Spirit who comforts them and countless more benefits for this life and life ever after.

Fear not his yoke; for his commands are holy, just, and good. His greatest command is to love one another, and Christ gave the ultimate example of how to love—sacrificially. If you haven't come to faith yet, Christ's yoke may appear hard. But in him alone, forgiveness and a right standing before God are freely granted by faith. Surely Christ's yoke is easy and his burden light.

VERSES TO REFLECT ON

Come to me, all you who are weary and burdened, and I will give you rest. Take my yoke upon you and learn from me, for I am gentle and humble in heart, and you will find rest for your souls. For my yoke is easy and my burden is light.

Matthew 11:28-30

MEMORY VERSE

It is for freedom that Christ has set us free. Stand firm, then, and do not let yourselves be burdened again by a yoke of slavery.

Galatians 5:1

IN YOUR OWN WORDS: HOW IS IT THAT CHRIST'S YOKE IS EASY?

_____

_____

_____

_____

_____

_____

_____

_____

_____

RESPONDING TO GOD IN PRAYER

_____

_____

_____

_____

_____

_____

_____

_____

ZION

Zion in Scripture is often used as a synonym for Jerusalem, and even more specifically of the mountain near Jerusalem. Zion was also the name of the temple mount within Jerusalem, which was the seat of the first and second holy temple. Zion's meaning broadened to God's eternal kingdom through the Old Testament prophets who foretold of a time of great joy when the Savior of Israel would appear in Zion at his second coming. With the temple and prophetic ideas in view, the New Testament authors envision Zion as the heavenly dwelling place of Almighty God.

The author of Hebrews penned it this way, "But you have come to Mount Zion, to the city of the living God, the heavenly Jerusalem" (Heb. 12:22). The writer declares repeatedly that there is only one road, one gate, one way that leads to Mount Zion, to the city of the living God. It is by faith in Jesus Christ alone. He is the preeminent one, the one for which the prophets of the Old Testament had been waiting. He is the Savior, and it is through him alone that the believer may roam the heavenly streets of Zion.

VERSES TO REFLECT ON

They shall ask the way to Zion, with faces turned toward it, saying, 'Come, let us join ourselves to the Lord in an everlasting covenant that will never be forgotten.'
Jeremiah 50:5

And in this way all Israel will be saved, as it is written, "The Deliverer will come from Zion, he will banish ungodliness from Jacob."
Romans 11:26

But you have come to Mount Zion, to the heavenly Jerusalem, the city of the living God. You have come to thousands upon thousands of angels in joyful assembly, to the church of the firstborn, whose names are written in heaven. You have come to God, the judge of all men, to the spirits of righteous men made perfect, to Jesus the mediator of a new covenant.
Hebrews 12:22-24

MEMORY VERSE

Sing the praises of the LORD, enthroned in Zion; proclaim among the nations what he has done.
Psalm 9:11

IN YOUR OWN WORDS: HOW IS ZION USED IN THE SCRIPTURES?

_____

_____

_____

_____

_____

_____

_____

_____

RESPONDING TO GOD IN PRAYER

_____

_____

_____

_____

_____

_____

_____

EPILOGUE

For God so loved the world that he sent his Son on an eternal rescue mission to earth. While he was on this planet, Jesus lived a perfect life, was rejected by men and was crucified. On the cross he bore humanity's sin, suffered God's wrath and died in our place. On the third day he rose from the dead, proving that the Father accepted his sacrifice for sin. Forty days later he ascended and now sits at the right hand of the Father, interceding for everyone who trusts in him. All who acknowledge and repent of their sin, and in faith embrace Christ for all that he is and has done, are pardoned by God. They are completely forgiven and declared righteous in God's sight, and are thereby fully accepted by him. This is the gospel of Jesus Christ. This is good news indeed.

Though this book briefly defines twenty-six facets of God's glorious gospel, there are countless more. Yet it is my prayer that God would use the good news of Jesus Christ presented here, and by the power of his Spirit your heart would be opened to believe. If you have already believed, may reading this book be an occasion for you to rejoice in all that our Savior is, and has done for you.

The consequences of not believing in Christ are far too great to ignore. It has repercussions not only for where you will spend eternity, but also for how fulfilled and purposeful your life will be here on earth. The good news is that God, in his abundant mercy and grace, has provided the very things that we need in order to be accepted by him—forgiveness and righteousness. What God demands, God supplies! Through his perfect life and sacrificial death, Christ alone is sufficient to give us what we desperately need and cannot attain any other way.

To be very clear, we can do nothing good enough to earn our way to God. If you have been taught, even by a church that considers itself to be Christian, that you can live in a way that will please God enough to accept you, you have been misled. The gospel according to Jesus is that all you can do is admit you have nothing to offer, and receive God's mercy, which he lavishly provides through the person and work of Christ.

Perhaps you are an atheist like I used to be, and have decided none of this really applies to you because you don't believe in God anyway. I would urge you to consider a simple analogy based on the physical and societal laws we interact with every day. Just because you don't agree with them or like them doesn't mean they don't exist or have consequences. The same could be said of the spiritual realm. Don't let yourself be deceived or ignore spiritual realities any longer. God exists and one day we will all stand before him and will be held accountable to his truth. When you die the truth will confront you face to face—I urge you not to wait until then. The consequences are much too grave and eternal.

Do you know and feel a gnawing emptiness, an endless cycle of trying to fill that void with something meaningful? You want something so bad and finally get it, or something monumental happens, and within a few days you're already over it and need the next fix. We are all born with this infinite, insatiable void and there is only one thing in the whole universe that can fill it—our holy, infinite, loving God! You can go on the rest of your life unsuccessfully trying to fill that emptiness or you can fill it to the brim with the eternal God and have true purpose in life.

A picture is sometimes helpful in bringing home a point. Within the pages of Scripture we see a beautiful image of how Christ covers us with his perfection. The Bible speaks of a robe of righteousness. Christ has the brilliant white robe of righteousness that is desperately needed and readily accessible to the penitent and faith-filled sinner. Imagine the sinner clothed in a black robe—that represents sin. The bad news, for us as sinners, is that God justly punishes sin. The wonderful news of the gospel is that when the sinner believes in Christ, his black robe of sin is mercifully taken by Christ, who paid for that sin with his life on the cross, and they are forgiven. At the same time, the white robe of Christ's righteousness is graciously wrapped around the repentant sinner so that God sees the perfect righteousness of Christ and accepts that person in Christ. That is the greatest, most loving and merciful exchange in the world!

Have you been forgiven? Are you hungering and thirsting for a righteousness you desperately need, don't have and can't earn? Turn to Jesus Christ and trust in him to provide all that you need. And if you receive him by faith, seek out a local Bible-based body of believers where you can worship, learn, serve, pray, fellowship and grow together in Christ.

Behold, what manner of love is this, that Christ should be arraigned and we adorned, that the curse should be laid on His head and the crown set on ours.

Thomas Watson (1620-1686)

Author

Kelly Havrilla lives in Plymouth, MI, with her husband David. They are both outdoor enthusiasts, love hiking in the Colorado Rocky Mountains, and enjoy spending time with family and friends. After a career in marketing at General Motors she has pursued a variety of creative endeavors. However, her greatest passion is the gospel. Over the years God has graciously opened numerous avenues into several local and international communities into which she and David have opportunities to minister and share the gospel. From this passion and desire was born the Gospel Glories project.

OTHER GCD RESOURCES

Visit GCDiscipleship.com/Books

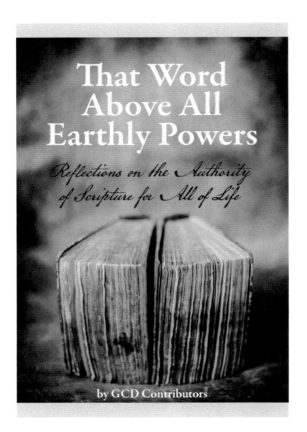

As the Protestant church celebrates the 500th anniversary of the Reformation the question of the authority and power of the Word of God for everyday life is still raised by many. Through this collection of essays, the Gospel-Centered Discipleship team seeks to demonstrate not only the rich theological implications of the authority of the Bible, but also the life-altering power of God's Word for everyday, ordinary life.

GCD's aim is to see the Word of God "make, mature, and multiply disciples of Jesus." As Martin Luther declared, " the Bible is alive, it speaks to me, it has feet, it runs after me, it has hands, it lays hold [of] me." He was announcing the power of the Bible "above all earthly powers."

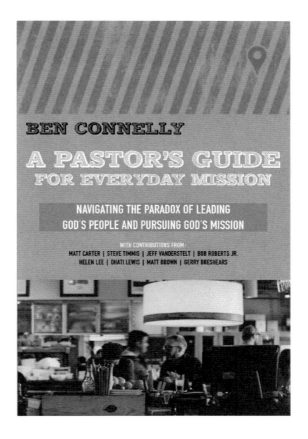

After fifteen plus years of vocational ministry, Ben Connelly had an epiphany. He had missed the great commission. He was really good at keeping Christians happy and really bad at making disciples. *A Pastor's Guide to Everyday Mission* helps those in paid ministry positions rediscover—and live—their life as God's missionaries, even as they minister to God's people.

We stand in the already and not yet. We are disciples serving between Christ's coming and his coming again. As we look backward, we see an astonishing baby boy cradled in his mother's arms and the saving life he will lead. Looking forward, we see a complete kingdom and restoration of all things. We celebrate Christmas only after grappling with the hope fulfilled and the hope still waiting.

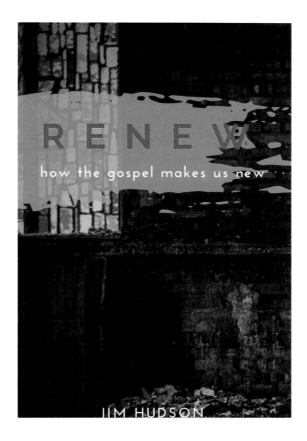

RENEW
how the gospel makes us new
JIM HUDSON

Too often we limit the power of the gospel to its blessings for us in the afterlife. We fail to see how the power of God, which raised Jesus from the dead, fuels our day-to-day battle against sin in this life. *Renew* shows us the grace of God is able to change us now.

For those looking to break specific sinful habits and temptations as well as those looking to gain a better grasp of how a Christian grows *Renew* speaks to the power of the gospel today.

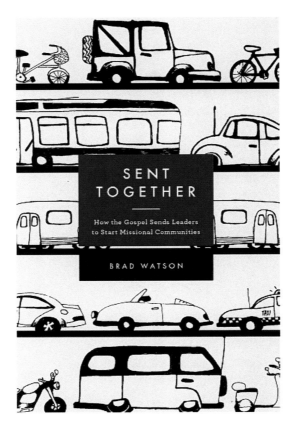

Jesus does not simply call us to be a lovely community together, but he sends us out to our neighborhoods, towns, and cities to declare and demonstrate the gospel. In fact, the gospel beckons men and women to take up the call of leading and starting communities that are sent like Jesus.

In *Sent Together*, Brad Watson helps leaders discover what it means to start communities centered on the gospel and mission. By exploring the gospel motivations that send leaders to start missional communities, Watson gives readers a framework for the purpose and ways of building a community that is deepening its understanding of the gospel, while also sharing it. *Sent Together* will serve as a field guide for leaders and training guide for those called to start missional communities.

Made in the USA
Monee, IL
20 January 2020